Baudelaire

Translated by
Laurence Lerner

PHOENIX
POETRY

This edition first published by Everyman in 1999
Phoenix edition first published in 2003

Introduction Translation and selection © J. M. Dent 1999
Chronology © J. M. Dent 2003

ISBN: 0 75381 744 6

Typeset by Deltatype Ltd, Birkenhead, Merseyside

Printed in China by South China Printing Co. Ltd.

A CIP catalogue reference for this book
is available from the British Library.

The Orion Publishing Group
Orion House
5 Upper St Martin's Lane
London
WC2H 9EA

Contents

Prose Poems

Introduction

The English reader may find it helpful to approach Baude-
laire through his great disciple T. S. Eliot. Eliot's essay on
Baudelaire, written in 1930, is an aggressive, even defiant,
rejection of liberal humanism. Admitting that he finds
Baudelaire a thoroughly perverse and insufferable person,
Eliot goes on to praise his awareness of evil. To portray the
sexual act as evil is 'more dignified, less boring, than the
natural, "life-giving" cheery automatism of the modern
world'; and 'the possibility of damnation is so immense a
relief in a world of electoral reform, plebiscites, sex reform
and dress reform, that damnation itself is an immediate
form of salvation . . . because it at last gives some signifi-
cance to living.'

This essay tells us a good deal about Eliot, especially the
Eliot of *The Waste Land*, but it also tells us something about
Baudelaire, for whom the world was often a waste land and
who certainly belongs to the long line of writers (too long,
some may sadly feel) who reject liberal humanism because
its view of man is too rational, too optimistic and too
superficial.

For Baudelaire the human heart offers little ground for
hope or admiration: it is an abyss, a volcano, a monster. And
so the very first poem, 'To the Reader', in *les Fleurs du mal*
begins by telling us that 'Stupidity and meanness, error,
vice, Inhabit and obsess us every one.' Against the normal,
the healthy and the rational, Baudelaire constantly sets

extreme, even perverted, experiences and devotes his poetry to exploring them. A rough list of the forms such extreme experience can take would include drugs, art, necrophilia, sex, spleen and travel: it is a list of the subjects of les Fleurs du mal.

First, drugs: their attraction is that they heighten sensibility, opening areas of experience that bourgeois normality excludes. The two drugs that interested Baudelaire were alcohol and hashish: one section of the volume is entitled 'Wine', and consists of studies of various kinds of frenetic experience, such as that of the drunken rag-and-bone man in the poem here translated as 'The Drunken Ragman' (le Vin des Chiffonners). Baudelaire devoted a fascinating book to narcotics, entitled les Paradis artificiels (Artificial Paradises), which describes how drug-induced dreams retain the particular tonality of the individual: they are a mirror, but a mirror which exaggerates. Interestingly, after some almost ecstatic descriptions of such dreams, he condemns the use of drugs, since they are an attempt to evade the necessary suffering of the human condition. 'Every man who does not accept the conditions of life sells his soul', for he is trying to escape from 'human liberty and its indispensable suffering'. The human condition is precious, above all, for its pain. 'Humanity is not so abandoned, so deprived of honest methods of attaining to heaven that we are obliged to have recourse to pharmacy and witchcraft.' This alternation between an obsession with, and a sober moral judgement on, extreme experiences is one clue to the paradox of Baudelaire.

What then are the other (more honest?) methods of attaining that intensity of experience which alone makes life worthwhile? The most obvious is art: and it is clear that Baudelaire valued art for much the same qualities as he would have valued wine and hashish if he had not felt obliged to disapprove of them: it is a way of causing us to live more intensely. This is quite explicit in his finest piece of art criticism, the essay on Constantin Guys called 'The Painter of Modern Life'. Guys was a friend of Baudelaire (he is only referred to by his initials in the essay) whose sketches and watercolours depict fashionable Parisian life. However, it is not his subject-matter which makes him important for Baudelaire, but the fact that he finds the ordinary a source of excitement: the artist is compared to the child and the convalescent. 'The child sees everything as *new*; he is always *drunk*' (compare the prose poem 'Get Drunk': *Enivrez-vous*). This is a doctrine similar to that of the great English Romantics. Coleridge praised poetry for 'awakening the mind's attention from the lethargy of custom, and directing it to the loveliness and the wonders of the world before us' – a doctrine caught up again by the twentieth-century structuralist view that the function of literature is defamiliarisation. Baudelaire's conception of sensibility can be seen as looking both backwards and forwards.

The most scandalous form of extreme experience sought out in *les Fleurs du mal* is necrophilia, the love of death, which crops up in poems on many subjects and sometimes takes centre stage. Baudelaire has his share of the Romantic death-wish, familiar to us in Keats and Shelley, the longing to cease upon the midnight with no pain, which protects against fear of death by investing it with a dreamlike seductiveness; but he also has something more shocking and indeed disgusting, a lingering on physical decay and rotting corpses (as in 'A Voyage to Cythera').

Necrophilia and sex are never far apart in Baudelaire; and sex is the most prominent theme in *les Fleurs du mal*. Almost half the poems are to or about women, and they range from conventional tributes to their beauty to a sometimes disgusted dwelling on corruption and decay. We know who some of these women were, but biographical readings tell us little of importance about the poems, which are concerned above all with the woman's beauty and the emotional needs of the poet. Sometimes the woman is seen as a prostitute the poet has fallen in love with: hence the air of corruption that so often lurks behind the praise. None of the love poems is more haunting than the marvellous poem 'Hair' (la Chevelure), in which the longing to escape becomes a perfect symbol for sexual surrender.

There remain two other forms which Baudelaire's longing for the extension of experience takes, spleen and travel. In writing of these, he is at his greatest; and perhaps there is no finer way into his poetry than the small group of haunting and highly individual poems, all called 'Spleen', and all expressing the same strange emotion. For Eliot, this emotion was 'a true form of acedia arising from the unsuccessful struggle towards the spiritual life'. 'Acedia' is an old term from moral theology, meaning torpor or weariness of a kind which destroys the spiritual life; and Eliot's remark reminds us of how profoundly this modern, sophisticated poet belongs in a much older spiritual tradition, that of the contemptus mundi, the Christian despising of the world.

What is meant by spleen? It is odd that we should need to look for a translation, for it is after all an English word, borrowed by Baudelaire. But so marked is the individuality of these poems that they can be said first to isolate, then to describe, an emotion never before so well understood. The nearest word in Baudelaire's vocabulary is ennui, but we cannot translate spleen by 'boredom', since there is an intensity of self-contemplation in these poems that is the very opposite of bored. Their method is to unroll before us a procession of images that identify, with the help of a sombre rhythm and occasional explicit comments, a state of being, a kind of spiritual dryness coupled with intensity of contemplation.

Finally, travel: this provides the longest and most ambitious poem of Baudelaire's, called, simply 'le Voyage' (the definite article is of course often used in French where it would be absent in English, and the appropriate translation of this title seems to me 'Travelling', or (as I have preferred) 'Voyages'. This poem contrasts those who travel through unhappy love, politics or maladjustment, with the 'true travellers', those *qui partent pour partir*, who set off for the sake of setting off: the longing to escape is too fundamental to be explained by particular causes. The poem moves into a dialogue in which the stay-at-homes question the travellers, asking them what they have seen. Here the irony becomes complex: at first the travellers are bored, then some of the fascination of the voyage creeps in, but they have to confess, in the end, that the most beautiful cities were those *que le hasard fait avec les nuages*, which chance made out of clouds. By putting in front of us the dramatic situation in which travellers and listeners sometimes despise and sometimes envy each other, the poem compels us to ask whether there is really anything magical about the exotic. As well as the contrast between real and imaginary voyages, there is the contrast between travel as escape and travel as self-exploration (the same issue that was raised in Baudelaire's discussion of drugs). And then, finally, along with the knowledge that we shall never, by travelling, find anything really new, comes the conclusion that there is only one voyage left, and by a supreme act of imagination (poetic salvation or final self-deception?) we can persuade ourselves that the voyage to death will satisfy us at last. The poem concludes with a death-wish in the central Romantic tradition, in which death, for once, is not physically disgusting, but the longed-for solution to a situation too hard for us to endure – perhaps a surprisingly traditional ending for what may well be Baudelaire's most complex and ironic poem. But ending with death is unquestionably important, since the poem is placed in a section of *les Fleurs du mal* called 'Death' – the final section, and Baudelaire placed it last in the volume.

Finally, a few words about the form of Baudelaire's poetry. I began by suggesting that the English reader might approach Baudelaire through Eliot; and I conclude by suggesting that he can also be approached through Swinburne. Eliot, of course, is the dominant modernist in English poetry and he learned a great deal from the French poets who followed after Baudelaire, producing a poetry so different from anything which went before as to appear new in kind: Mallarmé's careful destruction of syntax, Rimbaud's whirl of imagery, Laforgue's irony and the theories of Valéry all found their way into English poetry through Eliot. All these poets, according to Valéry, could not have achieved what they did without their reading of Baudelaire. No doubt this is true: Baudelaire lies behind much modern poetry and *The Waste Land* may well be the nearest thing to an English *les Fleurs du mal*: its first section actually ends with the last line of Baudelaire's introductory poem, *Tu, hypocrite lecteur, mon semblable, mon frère*: literally, 'You, hypocrite reader, resembling me, my brother' – a dramatic declaration of poetic allegiance that at the same time expresses a contempt for the reader comparable to what the travellers feel towards the stay-at-homes in *le Voyage*. But *The Waste Land* would have seemed a very strange poem to Baudelaire. It is thoroughly modernist, based on the belief that poetry is discontinuous with prose, that a poem should dispense with narrative and argument and do what only poetry can do, evoke emotion by the associative power of imagery, sound and form. Baudelaire's poems, however, do all that the modernism of

Pound and Eliot forbids a poem to do: they tell stories, they have a paraphrasable content, they name the emotion they are describing, they are all in regular rhyme and metre. Baudelaire is not a modernist, not even the father of modernism: he is more like its ancestor. At times his poems show a rhetorical, declamatory streak that to the English reader seems to hearken back even before the Romantics to the eighteenth century, since such declamatory effects went out of the best English poetry with the Romantics. This side of Baudelaire may be the least acceptable to us today, though it also informs some of his finest poems, such as the sombre and tragic *Femmes damnées* (here translated as 'Lost Women').

So after indicating the important ways in which Baudelaire anticipates modernism, it is perhaps right to end by returning him firmly to the middle of the nineteenth century. If we look for Baudelaire's appearance in English poetry in his own time, we shall find him in an earlier and less complicated disciple. Few nineteenth-century poets are more locked up in the plangent, melodious musicality of Victorian suggestiveness than Swinburne, though Swinburne was also the enfant terrible who shocked Victorian respectability. And when Baudelaire died Swinburne wrote a long, eloquent and suggestive elegy, which has all Baudelaire's musicality and none of his careful, sculptured meanings. It is hard to imagine how a poem could be so like and at the same time so unlike Baudelaire:

> For always thee the fervid languid glories
>   Allured of heavier suns in mightier skies;
>   Thine ears knew all the wandering watery sighs
> Where the sea sobs round Lesbian promontories,
>   The barren kiss of piteous wave to wave
>   That knows not where is that Leucadian grave
> Which hides too deep the supreme head of song.
>
> LAURENCE LERNER

Baudelaire

To the Reader

Stupidity and meanness, error, vice,
Inhabit and obsess us every one.
As for remorse, we find it rather fun:
We nourish it, as beggars feed their lice.

Repentance gets us nowhere: our sins cling.
Confession seems a handsome gesture – then
We find we're on the muddy path again.
A few cheap tears can't pay for everything.

Evil is like a pillow. Lay your head
On its enchantments: Satan Trismegist
Rocks you asleep, that subtle alchemist,
Turning your golden penance into lead.

The Devil holds the strings, and moves them well.
Nothing's too ugly for us: we don't flinch
From stink or darkness. Inch by reeking inch,
One step per day, we're on our way to Hell.

To kiss and chew an old tart's withered breast
Is all we can afford. Debauchery,
Our only pleasure, we take furtively,
Squeezing it like an orange to the last.

A million devils guzzle in our brain,
Chewing like worms. Each time we take a breath
It bubbles through our flooded lungs, and Death
Gives a choked cry; we drown, then breathe again.

On the drab canvas of our destiny
The lovely patterns made by hate, disgrace,
Rape, dagger, poison, sword, have left no trace.
The reason is, we are too cowardly.

Our vices are a zoo. They hiss and crawl,
They bark and yell: dogs, crocodiles and apes,
Clawing and grunting; writhing and sliding shapes,
Jackals and vultures. But amongst them all

The very worst, consumed with quiet scorn,
Makes no grand gestures, never screams, but can
Turn towns to rubble, make a mock of man,
Swallow the world in one enormous yawn.

His name is Boredom. He sniffs, wipes his eye,
Puffs on his pipe, and dreams of hangings. You
Know this dear monster, reader. Yes you do,
Admit it. We are brothers, you and I.

The Albatross

Ships on their long monotonous voyages glide
Over vast deeps, an albatross or two,
Graceful and indolent, following at their side.
The sailors having nothing else to do

Catch them and dump them helpless on the deck.
And so the one-time monarch of the skies,
Dragging its useless wings like oars, its back
Crippled and clumsy, flounders where it lies.

The sailors have their fun: one takes his pipe
And taps its beak, while others imitate
Its awkward movements, stomping round the ship.
How graceful once, how helpless now. That's fate.

The poet too glides swiftly through the clouds,
Haunting the storm: how happily he sings.
But down on earth among the hissing crowds
He trips and tangles in his giant wings.

Correspondences

Listen! They must be words, drifting between
These living pillars: elusive, never simple.
We walk through groves of symbols, dark and green,
Which smile and watch us. Nature is a temple.

Echo meets echo on the darkening ground;
They blend and fade to perfect harmony.
Scents answer colour, colours answer sound,
As darkness dazzles with its clarity.

Some scents are tender as a baby's skin,
Some delicate as oboes, some grass-green;
Others, that open on infinity,
Are brassy and corrupt and savoury
– Amber and musk, incense and benjamin.
They sing: all being is a unity.

The Beacons

Rubens, dark river, garden of repose;
Pillow of fleshly joy and chastity;
Unceasing life within you moves and flows,
Like air through air, or water through the sea.

Leonardo, sombre mirror, by whose aid
We can glimpse angels, watch the haunting lines
That play about their smile, within the shade
Of glaciers and strange landscapes filled with pines.

Rembrandt, a hospital: among the gloom
Lie piles of rubbish, from which tears and prayers
Ascend. A crucifix in every room.
Below, a ray of winter sunshine flares.

In the vague world of Michael Angelo
Hercules is identified with Christ;
Ghosts in the twilight rising from below
Tear at their shrouds as they unclench their fist.

Pert as a faun, bad-tempered as a bully;
Heart big with pride, and body weak and pale;
Lover of louts, Puget delights to sully
The world with hideous beauties from a jail.

Watteau: a carnival, where cavaliers
Glitter like butterflies with wings of pearl;
Delicate decor lit by chandeliers;
Madly beneath their blaze the dancers whirl.

Goya, a nightmare, full of the unknown:
A roasting foetus at a witches' revel;
Old women at the mirror; or bent down
To adjust a stocking and entice the devil.

Delacroix, lake of blood, shaded by firs,
Beneath an angry heaven, where deformed
And evil angels play mysterious airs.
A strangled sigh by Weber is performed.

These maledictions and these blasphemies
Echo through mazes, form a great Te Deum;
These cries, these sobbings and these ecstasies
Are for us mortals heavenly opium.

The cry goes up; a thousand sentinels
Repeat it, by a thousand voices borne;
A searchlight finds a thousand citadels;
Deep in the forest fades the huntsman's horn.

What better witness, Lord, could we provide,
Than this long sob, of human dignity.
It rolls from age to age; will not have died
Until absorbed into eternity.

The Sick Muse

Poor Muse, what's wrong? Your hollow eyes today
Are full of nightmare visions, silent, cold.
See, your complexion's red, then pale, then grey,
Reflecting fear and madness. Muse, you're old.

Have impish roses and green succubi
Tempted you in a terror-haunted sleep,
So that you dreamed yourself in Pompeii,
Trapped under ashes, fabulous and deep?

Couldn't you bring me something healthier,
More pure, more pious and more orthodox,
More fitting for a Christian to adore?

Couldn't you shape a true hexameter
Inspired by Pan, the god of harvests, or
Phoebus Apollo of the golden locks?

Muse for Sale

Dear Muse, I know you're fond of palaces:
So when in January the North Wind comes,
Your feet turn blue, and your blood starts to freeze,
Where will you find a fire to warm your bones?

The moon's rays struggling through the window pane
Will hardly warm you; and when funds run dry
As your mouth dries as well, the freezing rain
Won't turn to money tumbling from the sky.

To earn your bread you'll need to join the choir
And swing the censer as an altar boy
(Do you believe all that? They won't inquire),

Or else, a starving acrobat, conceal
Your tears, display your talents, leap and smile,
To melt the vulgar hearts of standers by.

The Enemy

My youth was filled with storms: dark thunderheads
Lit up by sudden sunshine. Wind and rain
Tore at my garden, left the ravaged beds
Stripped bare of soil. How few ripe fruits remain!

Now it is autumn: my ideas turn brown.
Look at the land: I'll need spade, rake and broom
To clear that flooded mess. The sodden ground
Is full of holes, each bigger than a tomb.

I dream new flowers now: but who can tell
If they'll take root in this exhausted soil?
The nourishment they need is strange and rare.

Time eats at life: no wonder we despair.
Our enemy feeds on the blood we lose.
He gnaws our heart, and look how strong he grows.

Ante-Natal

I must have lived once in a portico
With towering pillars, massive and upright,
Which glinted in the ocean's sunset glow
Like caves of basalt in the evening light.

Caught in the slow swell, images of stars
Moved to and fro in powerful harmonies;
Their colours sang to strange, elusive airs,
Blending with sunset in my dancing eyes.

Calm and voluptuous was that land: the waves
Beat on the splendid shore, while naked slaves
Perfumed and handsome, fanned my brow: their care,

Their only care, was, as the years went by,
As the sun crawled across the splendid sky,
To find my secret, to fan my despair.

Beauty

The poets love me: they adore my breast
And bruise themselves upon it, one by one.
Matter itself, though mute, will not outlast
Their love for me. I am their dream of stone.

I hate all movement. Understood by none,
A sphinx composed against the brilliant sky,
With heart of snow and body of a swan,
White joined to white, I neither laugh nor cry.

The attitudes I strike, and which derive
From all the world's great monuments, can drive
Poets to burn the midnight oil; to keep

Those docile lovers spellbound with surmise
I have two magic mirrors, pure and deep:
My eyes: my clear and beautifying eyes.

The Giantess

If I had lived in that wild early world
When each day saw new monstruosities,
I would have fawned upon a giantess, curled
Voluptuous as a cat around her knees.

I would have watched her soul and body both
Take form from her perverse, athletic joys,
Guessed at the sombre flames that lurked beneath,
Watching the wet mists swimming in her eyes.

I would have scrambled up her sloping thighs,
Explored her limbs – and when, some languid June,
She stretched beneath a hypochondriac sun
Along the fields, I would have slept as well
Casually shadowed by her drooping breasts
– A peaceful village underneath the hill.

Exotic Perfume

Eyes closed against the autumn heat, I lean
My head on your breast and dream of tropic strands,
Of the heavy smell that drifts from the tamarinds,
Of the slow caress of an exotic sun,

Of islands paced by slender, muscled men,
By girls with come-hither eyes and beckoning hands,
Where strange trees shake their strange fruits to the
  winds:
This is the world I enter, breathing your skin.

You smell of distance. Battered masts, and sails
Exhausted from their struggle with the deep
Crowd in the harbour as I drop asleep,
Feeling your breathing while my soul is winging
Its way above strange shores and distant hills.
Listen. Far off. Hark to the sailors singing.

Hair

The bedroom fills with memories as you shake
Your head and curls come rippling down your neck:
O golden mane, O perfumed nonchalance,
What passions waken as I stroke that fleece!

Another world lives in those depths: wild, far,
Fiery and languid: Asia or Africa.
Imprisoned in that aromatic tent,
I swim upon the music of your scent.

Somewhere, far off, sap flows abundantly
In men and trees: O sea of ebony.
Carry me there, dazzle me with your dreams
Of oars and masts and sails, of suns and flames.

I gulp the scents, the colours and the sound
Of a great port: the sea a golden ground,
The ships with open arms, the trembling air,
Eternal sunlight pouring everywhere.

An ocean lurks within the ocean of
Your tresses, and I dive, drunken with love,
In search of sloth and its fecundity.
Darkness encloses and caresses me,

A dark blue tent of hair that nonetheless
Reveals the sky, and twisting, tress by tress,
Intoxicates with odours – musk and tar
And coco oil, the perfumes of your hair.

I shall sow rubies, sapphires, diamonds, pearls
– How long? For ever! – in your heavy curls.
Never be deaf to my desires, but be
My dreams' oasis, a distillery
From which I drink long sips of memory.

The nightly heavens are not more beautiful

The nightly heavens are not more beautiful
Than you, beloved, sorrowful and still,
My vase of tears; and when you turn away
My love grows stronger. Night displacing day,
I love you for the leagues of irony
You place between my pleading and the sky.

I crawl across your body like a horde
Of worms across a corpse. O beast, adored
The more you show me, to augment my pain,
Your splendid and implacable disdain.

The Snake Dance

Stretch those indolent limbs, my dear;
  Breathe slowly in;
Perfect. I love to watch
  The shimmer of skin.

The sharp perfume of your hair
  As it tumbles down
Is a restless ocean: its waves
  Blue and fragrant brown.

My soul is a boat; at dawn
  Dreams are laid by.
It feels the breeze; sets off
  For a distant sky.

Those secretive eyes: nothing
  Bitter or sweet is told –
Jewels of ice in which
  Iron mingles with gold.

The rhythm of your walk
  Sways and entrances,
Suggests a wand round which
  A serpent dances.

Your childish head grows heavy,
  Sleepy, indolent;
Sways with the easy grace of
  A young elephant.

I watch your lovely body lean
  Sideways and dip
Its yardarms in the water:
  A delicate ship.

Waters fill your mouth,
  Wash over your teeth.
Glaciers are melting, filling
  It from far beneath.

I seem to drink Tokay,
  Powerful and tart,
A liquid sky which scatters
  Stars across my heart.

You Will Repent

Who understands the poet? Only the tomb.
So to the tomb I have confessed my dream.

My dark, my sombre beauty, when you lie
Asleep beneath black marble, when your rich
Mansion has turned to crumbling masonry,
Your bedroom to a dark and hollow ditch,

And when beneath the weight of all that stone
Your heart can neither wish nor even move,
Your thighs are locked, your feet no longer run
The gay voluptuous messages of love,

What will it profit that you never knew
What the dead weep at, you well-mannered whore?
Insomnia and fevers wait for you,
And worms will gnaw you as remorse might gnaw.

These verses are for you

These verses are for you, that if my name
Somehow survives the ravages of time,
Sets future readers dreaming, and if fame,
Swelling its sails, drive on my deathless rhyme,

Your memory, a fable from the past,
May tire the reader, beating at his brain;
And by a strange fraternal bond will last,
Tied to my poems, preserved in their disdain.

Outcast, who from the lowest depths of hell
To the ninth heaven, none cares about but I,
Shadow, and with a shade's fragility,

You spurn with glance and gesture undismayed
The mortal fools who think you bitter. Angel
With brow of bronze, statue with eyes of jade.

The Whole Lot

In my attic room this morning
The devil came to pay a visit.
He springs his questions without warning,
And so he said: 'Tell me, what is it

Among the objects black and pink
Which constitute their charming body,
Which of the beauties do you think
The finest? Tell me. Don't be shoddy,

Tell the truth.' Upon my soul
I said to His Malignity:
'All her qualities console
And enchant me equally.

How when all her charms delight
Can I be asked to pick out one?
She soothes my spirit like the night,
She dazzles like the dawn.

In harmony so wonderful
No one note can predominate;
It's much too intellectual
To pick on this one or on that.

O mystic metamorphosis
When senses interpenetrate.
The perfume: her voice gives us this.
The music: her breath brings us that.'

Evening Harmony

Evening has come: this is the languid hour
When sounds and perfumes quiver, mount and blend.
Notes of a melancholy waltz ascend.
The breeze draws incense out of every flower.

As sounds and perfumes quiver, mount and blend,
Trembling, the violins haunt us with strange power.
The breeze draws incense out of every flower,
And benedictions from the sky descend.

Trembling, the violins haunt us with strange power.
Deep darkness opens, stretching without end,
And benedictions from the sky descend,
Then disappear beneath a bloodsoaked shower.

Deep darkness opens, stretching without end.
Our memories guide us like a lighthouse tower,
Then disappear beneath a bloodsoaked shower.
Only your memory glows in me, dear friend.

Murky Sky

It seems that wreaths of vapour hide your eyes:
Even their colour difficult to surmise,
Reflecting the pale indolence of the sky:
Blue, grey or green? Tender or cruel or sly?

How you remind us of the warm white days
That wrap the heart in their bewitching haze
And leave us shaken by mysterious grief.
Can wakened nerves bring the drugged heart relief?

When the sun permeates the misty air
Horizons beckon, and I see you there.
You are a landscape bathed in misty light,
A murky sky which here and there turns bright.

Dangerous woman: climates that entice:
When winter comes with snow and rigid ice,
Will I still love you? Will the iron frost
Bring sharper pleasures than the year has lost?

Invitation to the Voyage

My child, my sister, we
Would know felicity
If we escaped to where
We could live together
In leisure that lasts for ever,
Your presence filling the air.
Damp suns in cloudy skies
Remind me of your eyes:
The glimmer that appears,
Haunting, yet treacherous too,
As their brilliant blue
Emerges out of tears.

It is a land of perfect peace,
Beauty and joy that never cease.

The antique furniture
That Time the polisher
Makes ready for our room;
The amber-scented hours
Filled with hothouse flowers
That drug us with perfume;
Mirrors on the walls
Where light from the ceiling falls
In oriental glory:
Calm order where the whole
Whispers to the soul
Its childhood story.

It is a land of perfect peace,
Order and calm that never cease.

On the canals afloat,
Look – boat after little boat:
How far they've come,
Sailing the seven seas
Only to please
Your every whim.
Sunsets enfold
In hyacinth and gold
Field, canal and town:
The boats drop asleep,
Dreaming of the deep:
Night settles down.

It is a land of perfect peace,
Beauty and calm that never cease.

Autumn Song

I love your shadowy eyes, your olive skin,
Your tender loveliness, but all's dark today.
Not home nor hearth nor even love can win
My thoughts from where the sunlight strokes the sea.

But mother me and love me all the same,
Sweetheart and sister: be that brief delight,
That glimpse of joy, ungrateful as I am,
That autumn gives before the fall of night.

Just let me lay my head upon your knees:
It won't take long: the grave is waiting; death
Allows one torrid summer. Now let's seize
The golden sweetness of its aftermath.

To a Madonna   Ex Voto in Spanish Taste

Madonna, mistress, may I build for you
An altar raised among my pain and woe,
And in the blackest corner of my heart,
Far from desire and mockery, set apart,
Construct a niche, enamelled gold and blue,
Holding a statue consecrate to you?
And with my lattice-work of verse, inset
With crystal rhymes, I'll make a coronet
To place, Madonna, on your mortal head.
And since I'm jealous I shall carve and spread
A heavy cloak 'around your breast and arms,
Lined with suspicion, to conceal your charms,
Embroidered not with pearls, but tears. Your dress,
Made out of my desires, will touch, caress,
And undulate about your body, kiss
Every protuberance of your warm flesh.
From my respect I'll make you shoes of satin,
To wrap your perfect feet, and keep their pattern
In every detail, like a faithful mould,
Grateful they had divinity to hold.
And if despite my art I try and fail
To carve a silver crescent pedestal,
Under your heels I'll place the snake instead
That bites my entrails: you can crush its head
Swollen with hate: it will not bruise your heel,
Redemptress, clad in virtue as in steel.
Glinting like stars upon the ceiling's blue
My thoughts arranged like candles gaze on you
With eyes of flame; they cast a pallid sheen
Upon the altar of the Virgin Queen.
My act of worship thrills through every sense

Turning to myrrh and musk and frankincense,
And rises like a vapour from below
To you on your cold summit, crowned with snow.

Finally, to fulfil your role as Mary,
To mingle love with some barbarity,
To play the hangman whom repentance wins,
I shall make daggers of the deadly sins,
Sharpen them well, and tie you to the wall,
Take careful aim at love, and send them all
Into the target, dart by dart by dart,
Into your streaming, panting, sobbing heart.

Sadness and Distraction

And tell me, Beryl, does your heart at times
Escape the oceanic urban mud,
Fly to another ocean, free from crimes,
A pale blue, virginal and sunlit flood?
Does your heart, Beryl, long for that sometimes?

The sea, the endless sea, our consolation,
Sighs hoarsely to the wind's accompaniment,
Performs its task of quiet celebration:
What demon gave it that sublime accent –
The sea, the endless sea, our consolation?

Carry me off, by air or sea or land,
Far from the city and its moral peril,
Far from this mud made out of tears and sand.
Surely your heart too must be crying, Beryl,
Carry me off, by air or sea or land.

How far that paradise must lie above
Our world, where somewhere in a clear blue light
All that we love is worthy of our love,
Where the heart drowns in unalloyed delight:
How far, how very far, it lies above!

But the green paradise that children knew,
Of races, nosegays, kisses, melodies,
Of hidden violins that play to you,
And jugs of wine at night among the trees,
– But the green paradise that children knew,

That paradise when all was innocent,
Even our furtive joys, has disappeared;
Our plaintive cries, our silver voices sent
Into the distance: they will not be heard.
That paradise where all was innocent!

The Revenant

Like an angel with wild eye
Back into your bedroom I
Will slip each night without a sound
Just as darkness comes to ground,

And, gipsy, you will feel my kiss
Cold as moonlight on your face,
And my arms about your neck
Will twist and slither like a snake.

When morning rears its livid head,
Turn, and find an empty bed!
All day long you'll feel the chill.
Let others murmur and caress,
Woo your youth with gentleness.
Terror: that's how I shall rule.

The Melancholy Moon

The moon is indolent tonight: she seems
A careless beauty snuggling in a heap
Of cushions, dropping slowly off to sleep,
Caressing her breasts gently as she dreams.

Along the silken surfaces of snow
Collapsing elegantly in a swoon,
She lets her pale gaze travel slowly down
The floral visions mounting from below.

And if occasionally she drops a tear
Shot through with rainbow colours, opaline,
Upon the waiting earth, some poet there,
Sleepless, as poets almost always are,
Catches it in his hollowed hand, and then
He hides it in his heart, far from the sun.

Cats

Lovers and scholars, the ardent and the prim,
As they grow older, ripen; and love cats,
Those gentle household gods, those powerful pets,
Afraid of draughts, and sedentary, like them.

If only one could break their pride, how well
These voluptuary lovers of the dark
Who seek out silent corners where fears lurk
Would serve to draw the chariots of Hell.

Look at them dreaming: how that attitude
Suggests the Sphinx, which also dreams, and lies
Stretched out upon the sands in solitude.

Their fecund loins house magic powers; and see!
Like grains of sand that glint elusively,
The specks of gold inhabiting their eyes.

Owls

Ranged on the branches of a yew,
Darting red eyes that never blink,
Like Gods to whom the world seems new,
Behold the owls. They sit and think.

For hours and hours they do not stir:
The sun moves slowly down the sky,
And darkness settles everywhere;
The last sad rays of daylight die.

The wise man learns, observing them,
That man, the victim of a will
Incapable of keeping still,

Is doomed to pay the penalty
Of never feeling quite at home,
Besotted with the transitory.

Music

Music's a sea of sound; and once afloat
My pale star calls;
Mist hangs or huge skies loom above my boat:
I raise my sails,

Breast forward, and lungs swelling in the breeze,
All muscles tight,
I climb the slippery backs of tumbling seas
Hidden by night.

Tormented like my vessel by the storm
I feel at ease;
But when the sea is calm and the sun warm,

The waters bright,
Then all I find in the unmoving air
Is my despair.

The Cracked Bell

On winter nights the church bells in the mist
Condense or blur, and listening in love-hate
I peer into the past and reminisce,
Beside the glow and shuffling in the grate.

O lucky bells, lifting your voice in prayer,
Full-throated and in tune. An old sentry
Will still keep watch and through the winter air
Old but untarnished, you call out. And me?

My soul rings false: for when it populates
The nights with forms my artistry creates
Out of my boredom, all we hear's the harsh
Rattle of some poor devil as he lies
Under a pile of corpses, by a marsh
Of blood; and writhes, and cannot budge; and dies.

Spleen I

I am as old as all the memories
That fill the thousand drawers behind my eyes
With old love letters, legal documents,
Verses done up in ribbon, musty scents,
Piles of receipts, and dusty locks of hair.
I am so old more secrets rot in there
Than in a thousand attics. What am I?
A cave, a pyramid, a cemetery,
Among whose corpses long worms crawl and stray,
Gnaw like remorse, while the moon turns away.
I am the room in which Miss Havisham
Sits brooding and remembering. I am
The roses drooping, the outmoded gowns,
The mouldy wedding cake, the croaking sounds
Of memory among the corridors
Inhabited by ghosts of buried fears.

The days go on for ever. Snow descends.
All round, the level landscape never ends,
Stretches on every side, indifferently.
This is a kind of immortality.
A granite Sphinx within me sits and stares
Into the desert air, vague mists of fear
Curling around its limbs. And when the long
Rays of the sunset touch its throat, the air
Of the Sahara trembles with wild song.

Spleen II

It rains all year in the oppressive land
Of which I am the young decrepit king.
My tutors bow and scrape on every hand;
I much prefer my dogs; but dogs no more
Than stag or falcon, horse or anything,
Amuse me now. My favourite dwarf can sing
Grotesque and filthy songs; I pay no heed.
My people die in herds around my door:
I do not care; I'm sick; on my huge bed,
Half smothered by the hanging fleur-de-lys,
I lie all day imagining I'm dead.

My harlots peel off stockings, show black lace,
Let the last garment linger; not a smile
Plays on the skull that serves me for a face.

I keep an alchemist: his subtle art
Can purify, refine, turn lead to gold,
But cannot purge the dross that clogs my heart.

I've even thought of killings, Roman style,
(One thinks about such things as one grows old);
But if my streets ran blood, and all the drains
Were gushing blood, it wouldn't thaw the cold
And frozen muck of Lethe in my veins.

Spleen III

When the low sky hangs heavy as a lid,
Pressing like boredom on our baffled sight,
Seals t'1e horizon and lets down a flood
Of tainted daylight, gloomier than night;

When earth becomes a dungeon, shutting in
Hope like a bat that darts and twists and falls,
Scraping the roof with head or timid wing,
Dislodging plaster from the rotten walls;

When the interminable lines of rain
Are stretched like prison bars before our eyes,
And a mute horde of spiders in the brain
Wrap their disgusting webs round consciousness;

Bells lose their tempers suddenly, leap high,
Screaming like ghosts, homeless and obstinate,
Flinging their furious noises at the sky.
No land no language owns the sounds they make.

No music and no drums disturb the air;
Black hearses slowly move across the soul;
Hope weeps, defeated; and see, King Despair
Plants his black flag upon the slopes of skull.

The Clock

Frightening, impassive, sinister, the clock
Raises his finger like a threat: Remember!
Your heart becomes a target: griefs past number
Aimed at its quivering centre, strike and stick.

Pleasure evaporates: will disappear,
Fade like a dancer as the stage goes dark.
Your joys are rationed: each one leaves its mark:
Devours you, and diminishes your share.

Three thousand and six hundred times an hour
An insect voice reminds you like a rhyme:
'I'm now.' Then, 'I am once upon a time –
A filthy tube through which your life will pour.'

'Souviens-toi. Remember.' Unsparing! 'Esto memor.'
(My metal throat speaks all the languages)
'Don't lose your chance, and don't be frivolous.
Extract the gold; treat minutes like an ore.'

Time is a gambler who can't stop. Remember!
He always wins and doesn't need to cheat.
The gulf is thirsty; sands are running out;
Day fades. The night draws in. It is December.

The hours will strike: Chance, the Divinity,
Or Virtue, your distinguished virgin spouse,
Or even Remorse, the last room in the house,
– Or everything, will say: 'Too late now. Die!'

Parisian Landscape

I need to live among the roofs and towers
Like an astrologer among his stars,
I need to dream (to write my pastorals)
Through solemn noises from the nearby bells,
And wake, and hear them still; lean out and see
The many-masted city under me,
Paris, my restless workshop: drainpipes, spires,
The endless sky in reach of my desires.

Windows and stars light up among the mist.
I lean and watch, my chin upon my fist,
Rivers of smoke ascend and merge: the pale
And blatant moon is pouring out her spell.
Year in, year out, I'll watch the seasons pass
– Spring summer autumn – staring through the glass,
Till winter spreads its white monotony;
Then close the shutters on my fantasy.

All night in dreams I'll pass through shimmering halls;
Fountains will weep from alabaster bowls,
Birds sing and lovers kiss beneath blue skies,
The sound of flutes makes palaces arise.
Winter can riot at the window pane,
I shall not lift my head, or hear the rain,
Drowned in the damp voluptuous atmosphere
Through which my childhood idylls reappear,
In which the sun that sets my thoughts on fire
Charges the heavy climate with desire.

The Swan

I

I thought of you today, Andromache.
That little river in whose glass appears
Your nobly tragic widow's dignity,
In which you weep, increasing it with tears,

You called it Simois. Everything's new
Around the Carrousel: is this my town?
Paris has changed, alas, as cities do:
Emotions last while buildings are pulled down.

That cluster of ramshackle huts, that pile
Of broken shafts and cornices half done,
Grass, puddle, concrete stained with mud and oil,
Odds and ends shining on the ground: all gone!

There used to be a zoo there, and I saw,
One cold clear morning, just as work began,
Next to the pile of detritus, from where
The dust was rising like a hurricane,

A swan that had escaped. It placed its feet
Painfully on the paving stones; they ripped
The webs; its plumage draggling on the street
It reached a dried up water course, and dipped

Its wings with nervous gestures in the dust.
That swan became a myth, opened its beak,
'Water, when will you rain?' it said: it must
Have seen the waters of its native lake.

It stared and stared at the ironic sky,
So cruelly blue. With head erect it stood,
Stretching its neck, shaking convulsively,
As if addressing a reproach to God.

II

The Paris that I know has gone, but I,
Watching new buildings rise in giant blocks,
Wonder what's changed: the same sad memory,
My melancholy rooted like the rocks.

Passing the Louvre I thought about my swan,
Its futile gestures and its sick desire:
And then of you, Andromache, alone
In foreign lands: another exile there!

You, once the wife of noble Hector, then
Dragged off by Pyrrhus, bent in ecstasy
Above an empty tomb; from man to man
Passed down: your life become an allegory

And then the Negress, wasted, thin, half-blind,
Dragging her feet through mud, her haggard eye
Trying behind the wall of fog to find
The splendid palms of far-off Africa.

I think of those who weep through endless hours,
Of all who've lost the irretrievable,
Suckled by Grief, the kindly she-wolf, all
The half-starved orphans, withering like flowers!

I too am lost; I too hear memories
Sounding like horns, far off among the trees.
I think of sailors stranded on the shore,
All exiled — and there are so many more.

Seven Old Men

Teeming city, city crawling with dreams,
Where spectres grab the passer-by at noon,
Mystery flows like sap in your tight veins,
And dingy yellow fog pervades your gloom.

One morning early, in the struggling light,
The mist prolonged the houses, till they all
Floated upon a swirling stream of white:
It was a decor like an actor's soul.

Feeling myself a hero, gritting my teeth,
Saying 'Cheer up' to an exhausted me,
I tensed my nerve and walked it, street by street,
Hearing the tumbrils clatter. Suddenly

An old man dressed in filthy yellow rags
That caught the colour of the rainy sky,
On whom it would rain money if he begged
Were it not for the evil gleaming in his eye

Appeared. His shifty eye seemed soaked in gall,
Winter grew colder when he looked at you.
He had the straggling beard, the bent back, all
The tokens of the archetypal Jew.

A limping quadruped, inverted U,
Not bent but broken, leaning on his stick,
As if he trampled corpses with his shoe
He shuffled awkwardly through snow and muck.

Another followed: stick and bearded chin,
Eyes, rags, bent back, were all identical.
I watched the ruffian and his gruesome twin
Limp off together to some unknown goal.

What plot, what god, what cosmic irony
Conjoined those two – no, three! I looked again.
Some evil chance had made a mock of me:
I counted seven sinister old men.

– Or rather, one old creature multiplied
To seven monsters knocking at death's portal.
It was no joke: I stood there terrified
And realised that they were all immortal.

I am convinced that if an eighth had come,
Another leering double, I'd be dead.
– Another Phoenix, self-engendered, dumb,
Inexorable, dire . . . I turned and fled,

And stumbled homeward, shivering, seeing double,
Drunk with despair, and all my being stirred,
And shut the door in terror on my trouble,
Wounded by mystery, hurt by the absurd.

My reason reaching for the spinning tiller
Grabbed and let go; it twisted viciously.
My soul was drenched. The tempest was a killer.
I was a dancing hulk on a vast sea.

Little Old Women

In the old cities, among winding roads,
Where everything enchants, including crime,
I often watch, obedient to my moods,
Strange and decrepit creatures, touched with charm.

These twisted shapes were women once; their worn
And frozen rags, their petticoats in holes,
Protect their scars, their broken limbs from scorn;
These humpbacks are still lovable, still souls.

They tremble when an omnibus roars past;
Lashed by the vicious wind, they cannot hide;
A once embroidered, tattered bag clutched fast
As if it held a saint's bones, to their side.

They trot like puppets jerked into position;
Like wounded beasts they drag themselves along;
They dance without desire, without volition;
The devil plays them like a carillon.

Out of their broken bodies gimlet eyes
Pierce, gleaming like deep puddles in the night
– A young girl's eyes, responding with surprise
To a fresh world that fills her with delight.

Old women's coffins, as you must have seen,
And those of children, often look the same.
Death has his jokes: so this is what they mean –
A clever, quaint and fascinating game.

So when among the teeming streets I glimpse
One of these feeble ghosts, I've often thought,
Watching the fragile being as she limps,
She's come full circle, looking for her cot.

Those eyes, those eyes! – unfathomable wells
Brimming with tears, mysterious and moist:
I peer into their coloured crucibles,
Which I, born to misfortune, can't resist.

II

Often I've watched them crawling home to rest.
One evening I remember, when the sun
Had torn a crimson wound across the west,
I watched one sitting on a bench, alone.

A military band with lots of brass
As often happens when the shadows fall,
Sent out its floods of sound across the grass,
Attempting to make heroes of us all.

There she sat, upright, proud and dignified,
Eagerly gulped the martial music down;
Like an old eagle's, her eye opened wide;
Her marble brow seemed ready for a crown.

III

You plod your Stoic uncomplaining way
Through urban chaos. Some were courtesans,
Some of you saints, some mothers. And today
Nobody knows you, who were household names.

Famous for grace and elegance you were,
And now you've come to this. A drunkard reels
Against you, grabs your waist with ruttish leer;
A young delinquent gambols at your heels.

Ashamed to go on living as you slink
Along the walls in fear: strange destiny!
Debris of womankind, upon the brink
Of non-existence: ripe for eternity.

From far away I watch you tenderly,
My troubled eyes fixed on your tottering feet,
As if I was your father. You don't see
My passionate and clandestine delight.

I watch it all: I see your wasted days.
Sombre or bright; your passions bloom anew.
My heart distends with pity as I gaze.
Your sins delight my soul; your virtues too.

I'm of your race. You are my family,
O senile Eves. And every night I bid
A long farewell: next day, where will you be?
I leave you in the fearful grip of God.

Evening Twilight

Evening has come, the burglar's friend, at last,
With all its charms. The sky grows overcast
Like a low ceiling as the light grows dim.
Man turns to wolf as darkness closes in.

Evening, the happy hour, longed for by those
Whose aching muscles only need repose
After an honest day's hard work. Relief
To those devoured by unrelenting grief:
The plodding scholar with his aching head,
The crippled workman crawling to his bed.
But noxious demons too wake up again,
Slowly and sluggishly, like business men;
They knock against the shutters as they pass.
The wind torments the lamps; and through the glass
The twisted shapes grow brighter, and then fade.
The streets light up with lust; the girls parade.
The antheap opens: down long corridors
The spies of lust crawl, mumbling with their jaws,
Through mud, to undermine the helpless town
– Armies of worms, that filch their food from man.

Each evening kitchens whistle; here and there
Theatres yelp, orchestras start to snore;
The cafés where we gamble and eat chips
Fill up with half-clad girls with painted lips,
Their ponces, muggers, thieves, who only see
What's in your pocket; gently, skilfully,
Force open doors and safes: on what they take
They and their moll can manage for a week.

Soul, stop and think a moment. Let the roar
Drift past, and shut your ears; this is the hour
When invalids get worse, when sombre Night
Grabs at their throat, and into the common pit
With them. That ward is full; and more than one
Will never sit and eat his soup again
Next to his hearth while his beloved wife
Looks on and watches
                              – to say nothing of
Those who've had nothing of domestic life.

Yes, I remember the house

Yes, I remember the house, I remember it all,
The heavy curtains and the whitewashed wall,
A battered Venus shivering in the trees,
Her plaster hands hiding her nakedness,
And every evening the descending sun,
Washing the roofs, the grass, the window pane,
Fell open like a sheaf, spilling its light
And watched us sit at table half the night:
We hardly spoke, watching the shadows crawl
Across the frugal board and into the hall.

The Nurse

You can forget your jealousy: my nurse,
Asleep at last, lies underneath the grass.
We ought at least to take her a few flowers.
For when October shakes down leaves in showers
Around her headstone, and the battered trees
Fill the quiet graveyard with their elegies,
What must she think of us, asleep in bed?
You wouldn't like it either, being dead.
Warm in our sheets we whisper all night long:
Eaten by nightmares, silent, shivering.
Inhabited by worms, they lie alone
And listen to the snow upon the stone,
And listen as the years flow by above.
No friend or lover comes to mend their grave.

And if one night, December wild outside,
I found her sitting gravely by my side,
If, while the fire sang to the frosty air,
I turned towards the wall, and she was there,
Unnoticed in my armchair, shrinking, bent,
Come back to brood, a timid revenant,
With her maternal eye upon her child
(No more a child, alas), what should I find
To answer her, my dead and pious dear,
Seeing those hollow eyeballs ooze a tear.

Mist and Rain

Autumn and winter and the mud of spring
Wrap us in clammy shrouds that steam and cling,
Lay us in tombs that disappear in mist:
These are the drowsy seasons I love best.

On this huge plain where the wind romps, and where
The weathercock grows hoarse in the night air,
Spurning the lukewarm pleasures of past springs,
My soul is free to spread its raven wings.

My heart is clogged with thoughts of death, is chill
With winter's touch. Its only pleasure now
Is staring at the mist, the rain, the snow,
The pallid dark that lasts all day, until
Worn out with grief, a blank sky overhead,
We drop asleep in twos on a chance bed.

Morning Twilight

Morning. The bugle sounds. The streetlamps shake
In the dawn wind. Slowly the houses wake.

A swarm of nightmares twisting their dark heads,
The adolescents disarrange their beds.
Throbbing and turning like a Cyclops' eye
My lamp is a red stain upon the day.
The soul beneath its weight of blood and bone
Enacts that conflict of the lamp and dawn.
The air is damp, with tears upon its skin;
It trembles; the breeze dries its face.
                                    A man
Throws down his pen; the woman turns her back,
Saying, 'Enough'. The chimneys start to smoke.
Stupid with sex, the whores upon their beds
Drop off to sleep, pale-eyed, with aching heads.
A beggar woman pokes the dying brands,
Rubs her thin breasts, and blows upon her hands.

Women in labour close their eyes in pain;
Their screams redouble as the day is born.
Like a consumptive sobbing in his chest
A cock crows somewhere, tearing at the mist.

The roofs are islands in a ghostly sea.
This is death's moment. Unremittingly
He walks the wards for victims, and they choke.
Young men in evening dress stroll through the park
Or step from taxis, tired with the night's work.

Dawn shivers as it slinks across the Seine,
Wearing its dressing-gown of pink and green,
And Paris, poor old horse, blinks its tired eyes,
Feeling the harness tighten on its flesh.

The Drunken Ragman

A run down district: quarrels, beggars, tarts,
Streetlamps whose flames leap up in fits and starts
Each time the night-wind batters at the glass
To light the knots of loungers as they pass,

And light that ragman clinging to the walls
As if he clutched at metaphors; he falls,
Gets up, ignores the laughter, shakes his fist,
And pours his heart out, happy solipsist,

In projects he announces to the skies.
He barks: a thousand soldiers turn their eyes.
He knocks down criminals, relieves the poor.
Glories in virtue and reforms the law.

Yes, each poor devil, with his household cares,
Bowed down by age and toil, grunts as he bears
His pile of filthy rags down lanes and mews,
Unnoticed in the trash the city spews,

And reaches home, perfumed with alcohol,
Followed by comrades, battle-scarred and pale:
Their long moustaches droop like flags. The air
Suddenly fills with flowers: banners appear

Magically waving: drums and trumpets sound,
The sun shines; cheering thousands cluster round;
Everyone worships them and chants their name
In a wild orgy of success and fame.

Wine like the golden river Pactolus
Dazzles humanity; bestows on us
Distinction such as drunken voices sing:
You might mistake it for a real king.

When God repented of the misery
Endured by those who suffer silently,
He gave one gift to lull and to console:
His gift was sleep. Man added alcohol.

The Drunken Murderer

My wife is dead: that's my release
  To drink as often as I like.
When I would come home penniless
  Her crying caused my heart to break.

Now I'm as happy as a king
  – Pure air all round, bright skies above;
I smile with joy, remembering
  That summer when we fell in love.

Tortured by thirst I need to drink
  Red wine by tombfuls to calm down.
What does that mean? Just stop and think:
  Enough to cause my wife to drown.

I threw her body down the well,
  Tore up the stones surrounding it
And threw them after; as they fell
  I kept on trying to forget.

I begged her by the vows we swore
  – From whose bonds nothing can deliver –
To try and build our love once more
  – The days when we'd get drunk together,

To meet me at a lonely spot
  One evening; and to my surprise
The crazy woman came: (she's not
  More crazy than the rest of us.)

Although she was worn out and ill
　　She'd kept her looks; and that was why
Perceiving that I loved her still
　　I told her that she had to die.

No one can understand. Who'd think,
　　Among that morbid stupid crowd
Of layabouts undone by drink,
　　That wine could be a kind of shroud?

What tramp or bum or drunken lout,
　　Insensitive as a machine,
Has got the least idea what
　　Being in love can really mean?

It means black magic; poison, tears,
　　Processions of the newly dead,
Corpses that rise up from their biers
　　And shake their chains and nod their head!

So now I'm all alone – and free!
　　Tonight I'll drink till I pass out.
Fear and remorse will let me be;
　　I'll fall asleep upon the street,

Sleep like a dog and not wake up;
　　And if the wagons trundling by,
Laden with stones and mud, don't stop
　　I'll know I really ought to die:

Roll on, roll on: what do I care?
　　Cut me in two, or crush my head.
The whole thing doesn't mean much more
　　To me than devil, altar, God.

Lost Women

Sinking in perfumed cushions, Hippolyte
(The pale lamp offering a languid light)
Lay back and dreamed about the fierce caress
That led her youth from candour into bliss.
Like ocean travellers staring backwards for
The harbour that they left the day before,
Her eyes were seeking, reddened and intense,
The lost horizon of her innocence.
Her sluggish tears, her shattered look, her sad
Voluptuousness, her arms across the bed
Like useless weapons flung aside – how all
Served only to make her more beautiful!
Stretched at her feet, calm and relaxed, Delphine
Lay brooding with fierce eyes upon the scene
– A lioness who's pounced, and starts to play
Gaily with her already bleeding prey.
Two beauties: the one frail; the other, strong,
Who kneels in pride; and stretches; and takes long
Voluptuous sips of triumph at the shanks
That she has torn, as if requiring thanks.
The silent canticles of pleasure lie
Somewhere deep buried in the victim's eye.
She searches: for somewhere behind the lid
Lurks a sublime, mysterious gratitude.
'My Hippolyte, now do you understand
Why it requires a soft and gentle hand
To pluck the rose, to oil and push the gate,
And lead you through, blushing initiate?
Men ride us like a coach and six; they rush,
Planting their hooves across the tender flesh.
Look at me! Turn your face! O Hippolyte –

My soul, my heart, my sister, my delight,
Show me the magic in your sparkling eyes
And I will teach you darker, deeper joys.'
But Hippolyte lifted her youthful head;
'I'd do it all again, Delphine,' she said.
'I'm not ungrateful, but I am afraid.
It was a kind of orgy that we had.
Terrors descend on me in fearful hosts
And black battalions of scattered ghosts;
They seem to drive me down a moving road
Towards a low horizon filled with blood.
What have we done? Was it unnatural?
What is this strange misgiving that I feel?
I felt a shudder each time I was kissed.
But when I see your mouth I can't resist.
Don't look at me like that: it frightens me.
I love you. You are my affinity,
Even if you're a trap, I'll love you still,
Even if you're my entrance into Hell.'
With savage eyes, and voice intense with heat,
Striking the iron tripod with her feet,
Delphine replied, clutching her hair with hands,
'Hell is a word no lover understands.
I curse the dreamer whose stupidity
Attempts to mingle love and honesty.
Go. Find a husband. Find some brutal man,
Tell him you're his; let him do what he can;
Then with your bruises, like stigmata, creep
Home to me, show them, then repent and weep.
You can't serve God and Mammon: forget God.'
But seized by sudden grief the young girl said
'My deepest self is being torn apart.
A huge abyss has opened: it's my heart.
A crater spewing smoke has opened wide;

A monster who will not be satisfied
Devours my flesh and is devoured in turn
By Furies; I can feel their torches burn.
Come, draw the curtains. Secrecy is best.
We're both exhausted and it's time to rest.
Shut out the world. Open your arms. Make room.
Your flesh exhales the freshness of the tomb.'

Down, down, poor creatures. Down the slippery slope,
The broad and beaten road away from hope!
Once on the path to Hell no one turns back.
Puddles of crime lie seething round the track.
Faster and faster down the steep descent,
As pleasure is transformed to punishment.
No ray of light will penetrate the deep
Miasmic caverns where one finds no sleep.
The fearful perfumes of concupiscence
Torment the nostrils and corrupt the sense;
A bitter taste pervades your ecstasies,
Your skin grows hard, your thirst intensifies.
That is the future: flesh like bits of rag
Flapping and drooping like an old torn flag.
To run like wolves, far from humanity,
Through empty lands: that is your destiny.
For your lost souls there can be nothing new:
The infinity you flee from is in you.

The Bloodspring

Sometimes I feel my veins are leaking blood,
Rhythmic as tears. I feel the steady flood:
It bubbles like a spring. I hear the sound
But always grope in vain to find the wound.

It streams through Paris: every passer-by
Drinks, is refreshed. Each street's a river-bed,
Each pavement is an island, green and dry,
Lapped by this lake that stains all nature red.

How can I make these shapes of fear lie down?
I took to drink, tricked by its speciousness,
And eye and ear grew more alert, not less.

I looked for sleep in love's oblivion,
And found a bed of nails; my torn flesh burst,
My blood leaked out to slake those hussies' thirst.

A Voyage to Cythera

The sky was cloudless: bathed in sun, the boat
Was a bright angel: I felt my glad heart soar,
Glide like a bird around the rigging, float
Inebriate in air.

            – What is that shore,

That strange, dark island? – That is Cythera.
Surely you know it, famous in poetry,
The dream isle of the ageing bachelor.
– That? Is that all there is to see?

Cythera, mystic home of Aphrodite
In ancient times: does her ghost float above
Its waters still, mysterious and mighty,
Filling all hearts with languor and with love?

Island of blossom, worshipped by every nation,
Of myrtle and secrets and love's festivals,
The sighs of hearts breathed out in adoration
Hanging like incense over the flowering hills,

Or like a dove complaining from its bough.
Look at it: rocks, an occasional sharp cry,
An empty wilderness – that's Cythera now.
And yet one striking object caught my eye.

Was it a temple in a bosky grove
Where the young priestess, wandering through the
   trees,
On fire with barely sublimated love
Opens her robe to the caressing breeze?

No. Cruising down the coast, hugging the land,
Our sails disturbed the birds; they scattered high.
And then we saw it, like a cypress, grand:
A three-pronged gallows, dark against the sky.

A body hung there, ripe; and birds of prey
In clusters screamed and clawed and fought to slake
Their thirst on blood, their hunger on decay,
Each tearing, stabbing, with its filthy beak.

Out of the belly, ripped and gaping wide,
Intestines dangled; there were holes for eyes.
And, stuffed and gorging on their hideous food,
They'd found the morsel in between his thighs.

And troops of vermin underneath the feet
Sniffing and chewing, scampered here and there.
One of them, bigger, seemed to dominate
As if he was chief executioner.

Native of Cythera, born under this blue sky,
Deprived of burial, you deserved your fate,
Bearing these final insults silently.
What were the sins you had to expiate?

Ridiculous you hung there, while I stared
And felt the nausea rise. A flood of gall
Beat at my teeth. What you endured, I shared.
Ancient disgrace, and pain: I felt it all.

I saw the savage beaks, the jaws of steel,
As crows and panthers rose before my sight,
Brought back the terrors that I used to feel
When they devoured my flesh with such delight.

That perfect summer day of sky and sea
Had all turned dark: the air was dripping blood.
My heart was buried in an allegory,
I felt that I was sweating in a shroud.

So I have been to Cythera, and found
Myself upon a gallows: through the isle,
Nothing else standing on that holy ground.
God give me strength to contemplate my soul.

St Peter's Denial

Anathemas rise up in floods toward
The ranks of seraphim surrounding God.
What does he make of it? We curse, we cry:
He treats it as a kind of lullaby.
He sits there like a tyrant, swilling wine,
And listens to our symphony of pain.

Jesus, remember how you prayed all night
And no one heard you? Oh, God heard all right.
Remember how they hammered, the nails tore
Your flesh? God laughed, and asked for more.

You simpleton: to kneel, expecting grace!
Soldiers and kitchen maids spat in your face.
Your head, once filled with love, now crowned with
  thorns,
Your broken body dragging at your arms,
You hung, a target for the public gaze.

Did you dream then about the happy days
When you believed you had been sent by God,
When, mounted on that docile ass, you rode
Through flowers and palms, among the cheering
  crowd,
Or when, with hope and courage in your heart
You cleansed god's temple, drove the merchants out?
If you remembered all those moments then
Your bitterness was greater than your pain.

When my time comes I'll go without regret
Out of a world where dreaming means defeat.
To perish by the sword: that is my whim.
Peter denied you thrice. Well, good for him.

The Poor Praise Death

One thing consoles; one thing from day to day
Makes it worthwhile to take another breath,
To go on trudging on our endless way;
Only one thing: life's sole elixir, death.

Snow falls; gales blow; and dimly we make out
Against the darkness, real though far and small,
The always open inn we've read about,
That offers comfort, bed and board to all.

Death is an angel teaching us to dream;
It smooths our bed, it helps us to undress;
Electric fingers bring us ecstasy,

And open doors into a secret room.
Death is the porter of our ancient home;
The gateway to eternal nothingness.

Lesbos

Mother of Latin games and Greek delights,
Lesbos, where kiss on languid, lingering kiss,
Warm is the sun and fresh as fruit invites
To glorious days and long nights touched with bliss;
Mother of Latin games and Greek delights.

Lesbos where kisses shower like waterfalls
Descending unafraid to hidden deeps:
The water bubbles, slides, explodes and swirls
Gives quiet gurgles, hesitates and leaps:
Lesbos where kisses shower like waterfalls.

Lesbos where courtesan lures courtesan,
Where every sigh evokes an answering sigh;
Another Paphos glowing in the sun,
Sappho not Venus drawing every eye!
Lesbos where courtesan lures courtesan.

Lesbos, where nights are languorous and warm,
Where nubile girls with dark and deep-set eyes
Gaze in the mirror, while with loving palm
They stroke their sterile and voluptuous thighs;
Lesbos, where nights are languorous and warm.

Let Plato frown, old killjoy: you are queen
Of a huge empire in which every sense
Enjoys delights the world has seldom seen.
Excess of kissing is its own defence.
Let Plato frown, old killjoy: you are queen.

Ambitious hearts are martyred constantly,
And in that simple fact lies your excuse.
A radiant smile, glimpsed in a distant sky:
That is enough to put an end to us.
Ambitious hearts are martyred constantly.

What God would dare to judge you and condemn
Your pallid brow unless his golden scales
Could weigh the flood of tears that every stream
Bears to the sea from all your hills and dales?
What God would dare to judge you and condemn?

Just and unjust: who cares about such laws?
Large-hearted virgins, honour of the isle,
You have your own religion, your own cause:
Love laughs at such ideas as Heaven and Hell.
Just and unjust: who cares about such laws?

Lesbos from out the whole wide world chose me
To sing its secrets, compare girls with flowers.
While still a child I knew the mystery
Of frenzied laughter interspersed with tears.
Lesbos from out the whole wide world chose me.

Since then I've watched from the Leucadian rock,
A faithful sentinel with steady gaze,
Staring at every frigate, ketch or brig
That quivers in the distant azure haze;
Since then I've watched from the Leucadian rock,

To find out if the sea is merciful
And 'mid the echoing sobs the rock has kept
Will give us back one evening on the swell
The corpse of much-loved Sappho, she who leapt
To find out if the sea is merciful.

Sappho the poet, the lover and the male,
Although a woman: dark eyes flecked with black.
More beautiful than Venus, sad and pale:
Her black eyes hold a charm that blue eyes lack:
Sappho the poet, the lover and the male.

More beautiful than Venus as she stands,
Confronts the world, invites us to admire
Her youthful glory worshipped in all lands
Daughter of Ocean, ringed by the sun's gold fire:
More beautiful than Venus as she stands.

Sappho who died the day that she blasphemed
Against the rites of Lesbos, when she gave
Her lovely body over to be maimed
By a proud brute, like common passion's slave,
And died upon the day that she blasphemed.

And Lesbos has lamented since that time,
Though honoured and remembered everywhere;
Wild cries of horror at that primal crime
Rise to the heavens from its barren shore,
For Lesbos has lamented since that time.

The Jewels

Naked at last she moved towards me wearing
Only her echoing jewels (she knows my heart).
Her slow and arrogant step gave her the bearing
Of an Arab slave exulting in her art.

That shining world of stone and metal threw
Its sprightly and ironic music round.
Ravished, I watched; while my excitement grew
My ecstasy took shape as light and sound.

She laid her beckoning body out for love;
Smiled gently from her cushions: far below
The waves of passion broke; from high above
She watched them break, impetuous and slow.

She kept her eyes upon me, slow, intense;
She tried a pose or two: a tiger tamed!
Her charm a blend of lust and innocence,
Her movements casual, drowsy, unashamed.

The metamorphoses of lust! Arm, thigh,
Leg, belly, breasts, like grapes before me spread,
Disturbed my shrewd serenity of eye,
Writhed like a swan upon the oily bed.

Angels of Hell drew near me when she smiled,
Coaxing my soul to leave the calm remote
Withdrawn security in which it dwelt,
And smashed the crystal throne on which it sat.

The thigh and belly of Antiope,
Ephebe's breast and chin, compose a fresh
Unprecedented work of art: and see!
How the rouge glows upon that tawny flesh.

The weakening lamp resigned itself to die:
Only the hearth's flamboyant breath withstood
The darkness; and each time it heaved a sigh
It drenched her gold and amber skin with blood.

The Abyss

Yes Pascal too
Whichever way he turned, saw the abyss:
Word action dream desire all come to this.
Often I've felt a chilling wind that blew
From below consciousness.

Silence below,
Silence around, above, the silent shore,
The silent spaces with their fearful lure . . .
Hid in my dreams God shapes what all dreams show,
Dark symbols of desire.

I am afraid of sleep,
Afraid of it as one might be afraid
Of some enormous hole: where does it lead?
I stare through windows at infinity,
Longing for death's insensibility,
Or for a world of Form and Being, made
Not of the winds that blow from that strange sleep
Nor any part of me.

Meditation

Hush-a-bye, grief; don't fret; you wanted night
And, look, it's here; it's coming; street by street
Paris is wrapped in shadow – bringing sleep
To those who're lucky: the unlucky weep.

Sweating for Pleasure while he flicks his whip,
That crowd of hedonists, the urban mob,
Flock to obey their executioner.
Not that way, grief; give me your hand, come here.

And watch the dead years stroll the sky, and lean
Over the balustrades in crêpe-de-Chine;
And while the dying sunlight drops asleep
In corners, the sky thickens, while Regret
Smiling and shrouded, rises from the deep.
Listen, my darling, listen to the night.

Death and the Lovers

Divans as deep as tombs; delicate scents
Hovering round our beds like mysteries;
Flowers on all the shelves, fragrant, intense,
That opened just for us beneath strange skies;

Two torches and two mirrors: the flames vie,
Reflecting one another. Our two hearts
Are also mirrors, also flames. Each spurts:
One final flare-up, then the embers die.

One mystic evening, blue and pallid red,
A single lightning flash from each of us
Will burst like a long sob. They'll meet, and greet,

And then go out; and slipping through the gate
An angel takes the mirror, polishes,
And fans the embers that we thought were dead.

Death and the Artists

How often must I shake my bells and kiss
Your forehead, gloomy and grotesque: for ever?
How many arrows must I shoot and miss,
Aiming at Nature's mystery, you my quiver?

We might break many a clumsy armature,
We wear our spirit out in subtle schemes,
Before we get to contemplate the creature
We long for, sobbing in infernal dreams.

Some seek an idol they will never know,
And sculptors carrying the mark of Cain
Who hammer their own breast and their own brow

Long only for one strange and sombre prize:
That when like a new sun Death fills the skies
The flowers at last will blossom in their brain.

Voyages

I

Children pore over maps, night after night,
Building a world of wishes, lovingly.
By lamplight, how the world seems infinite
– How tiny by the light of memory!

One morning we set off, the mind on fire,
Heart big with rancour and hostility,
Confining, as we feel the swell mount higher,
Infinite longing to the finite sea,

Some running from a government, and some
From nameless traumas formed in infancy;
And some, the lovers, the star-gazers, from
A bed that as they slept became a sty.

Fleeing the Circean metamorphosis
They gorge on light and space and glowing skies;
The bite of ice, the bronze of sun, efface
The shame of sex in their neurotic eyes.

But the true travellers are those who go
Just for the sake of going, hearts at ease;
Their destiny their luggage. They don't know
What strange compulsion drives them to far seas.

These are the ones whose dreams drift through the sky,
Shapeless as clouds, elusive as a flame,
Conscripted to the search for some vast joy,
So strange that language offers it no name.

II

We're tops that spin; we're balls that bounce; we dance
Even in sleep. Curiosity leads us on –
An angel gloating as the puppets prance,
A cruel angel, lashing at the sun.

The goal we chase will not keep still: strange fate!
Where is it? Nowhere. That means everywhere.
We search for rest, and then accelerate,
Driven by Hope along our mad career.

The soul's a schooner, seeking the New World.
'Watch out!': the words come echoing from the deck.
Down from the crow's-nest other words are hurled:
'Love ... Fame ... Delight ...': the preludes to a
  wreck.

The lookout sees Utopias, isles of gold.
Imagination whispers to him: 'Knock,
And see the future open, worlds unfold.'
When morning breaks the ship has struck a rock.

How should we treat that lunatic who raves,
Sees Paradise, invents America?
Clap him in irons? Or toss him to the waves?
Poor fool, whose dreams make drowning bitterer.

An old tramp stumbling through the muddy lanes,
Sniffing the air to dream of paradise,
Sees fairyland behind the window panes.
The street's a slum to those with open eyes.

III

Travellers, tell us your tales. Deep in your eyes
We read of undersea marvels. Play us your tapes,
Open your caskets, packed with memories,
Show us your jewels, paint us those vast seascapes.

We want to travel too. We have no ship,
No plane, no ticket. Stuck at home and bored,
You're all we have. Breathe on our sails. Describe
The stars, the enormous spaces, you've adored.

Tell us, what did you see?

IV

                            Stars. Waves. Foam.
The usual. Shipwrecks. There were shocks galore.
Sunsets. Adventures. Memories of home.
Often we said to each other, What a bore!

The splendour of sunlight on the violet sea,
The splendour of sunset behind the silhouette
Of distant cities, brought anxiety
Mingled with longing to plunge where that bright sun
  set.

But none of the cities, none of the landscapes could
Ever equal the magic of those that our fancy drew
In the changing and dissolving shapes of cloud.
And the more we longed, the more our anxiety grew.

For fulfilment only increases desire: desire,
That old tree, fed by pleasure, taller than
The cypress. As the bark grows tougher, higher
And higher the branches stretch towards the sun.

Will it go on growing for ever? Perhaps it will.
Meanwhile, brothers, dreamers who stay at home,
Since you're convinced that exotic means beautiful,
We've brought you pictures to paste in your album.

We've worshipped idols, knowing they were fake;
Seen thrones of diamonds, watched each facet gleam,
Seen fairy palaces, whose pomp would make
Bank managers shudder even as they dream.

Intoxications of exotic dress,
Women who paint their nails and teeth and lips,
Accomplished conjurors, whom snakes caress –

V

Go on, go on, go on –

VI

No, friends, grow up.

We ought to tell you that we haven't yet
Mentioned the most important thing of all
(And the most boring): sin. We can't forget
That universal presence of the Fall:

Women, vile slaves, proud, stupid, who adore
Themselves without disgust or irony;
Men, greedy tyrants, rivers in the sewer,
Slaves of the slave, obsessed with lechery.

Religions everywhere – all like our own:
Ladders that point to heaven. Sanctity
Which wallows on a bed of nails; a groan
Of pleasure as it savours agony.

Mankind, the chatterbox, looking for trouble,
Sure of his genius, boasting his fill,
Calls out to God: 'My master and my double,
I recognise you. Damn you unto Hell!'

The least mad choose dementia; while the flock
Are rounded up and kept indoors by fate;
They fill a pipe with opium, and smoke.
And that's the world: we've finished our report.

VII

Travel broadens the mind. And what we learn
Is bitter ashes: that the world is tiny
And always was, and will be. We, in turn,
Are poisoned lakes in a vast tract of ennui.

Shall we set off? or stay? Go if you must,
Stay if you wish: it makes no difference.
Time is a sentry with his eye on us:
No one eludes his sombre vigilance.

Some in a frenzy, like the Wandering Jew
Or the Apostles, race from clime to clime,
Wriggle from under the deadly net. Some, too,
Never leave home, but manage to kill Time.

One day we'll feel his foot upon our neck,
And throb with hope, shouting 'Excelsior!'
Just as we used to race about the deck,
Hair loose in the wind, eyes on the Polar star,

This time we'll board a different boat, but bring
The same glad heart, to sail for Darkness. And
Listen: you hear the siren voices sing
Inviting us: 'This way to Lotus land.

This way to the happy harvest, to the gleam
Of everlasting bliss, the perfumed swoon;
This way to heart's desire; drift in a dream
To the country where it's always afternoon.'

I know that voice. I recognise the stark
Shape of the friend who beckons from afar:
'Your love, your sister's waiting. In the dark
You'll find your childhood. Steer for yonder star.'

VIII

Death, you old skipper, it is time to start:
Anchors aweigh. We're bored: we'll go and pack.
You know us well: hopeful, and glad at heart,
Though sky and sea are lowering and black.

Pour us a dram of poison: wish us well.
Our brain's on fire, and all we want to do
Is dive into the gulf – to Heaven or Hell,
We don't care which, as long as it is new.

PROSE POEMS

The Clown and the Venus

What a splendid day! The huge park lies exhausted under the burning eye of the sun, like youth under the domination of love.

No sound expresses the universal ecstasy; the waters themselves seem lulled to sleep. How different from human festivities: this is a silent orgy.

One would think that an ever-growing light causes the objects to sparkle more and more: that the excited flowers are burning with the desire to compete with the blue of the sky by means of the energy of their colours, and the heat, making the scents visible, is causing them to mount to the stars like smoke.

But in the midst of this universal pleasure, I perceived an afflicted creature.

At the feet of a colossal Venus one of those so-called fools, one of those willing clowns charged with the task of making kings laugh when Remorse or Boredom possesses them, accoutred in a striking and ridiculous costume, with horns and bells on his head, crouching against the pedestal, lifts his eyes, full of tears, towards the immortal goddess.

And his eyes say: – 'I am the last and loneliest of humans, deprived of love and friendship, and, because of that, inferior to the most imperfect animal. Yet I too was made to understand and feel immortal beauty. Oh Goddess! Have pity on my sadness and my delirium.'

But the implacable Venus stared at something in the distance with its marble eyes.

Crowds

It is not given to everyone to take a bath of multitude: enjoying the crowd is an art, and in order to indulge in a binge of vitality at the expense of the human race you need to be someone to whom, in your cradle, a good fairy gave a taste for disguise and for masques, a hatred of home, and a passion for travel.

Multitude, solitude: for the active and fertile poet, these are equivalent and convertible terms. He who does not know how to people his solitude does not know, either, how to be alone in a busy crowd.

The poet enjoys the incomparable privilege that he is able at will to be himself or someone else. Like wandering souls in search of a body, he can enter anyone's personality whenever he wishes. Only for him is everything vacant; and if certain places seem closed to him, it's because in his view they're not worth visiting.

The solitary and thoughtful walker extracts a singular intoxication from this universal communion. He who is easily able to marry the crowd knows a feverish bliss eternally denied to the egoist, closed up like a trunk, and the indolent, shut in himself like a mollusc. He is able to take on as his own all the professions, all the joys, all the sorrows that circumstances offer him.

What men call love is something thoroughly small, limited and weak, compared to that ineffable orgy, that holy prostitution of the soul, which gives itself entirely, poetry and charity, to whoever appears unexpectedly, to whatever stranger passes by.

It's good to teach the happy ones of this world, if only to humiliate their stupid pride for a moment, that there are forms of happiness superior to theirs, vaster and more refined. Those who found colonies, pastors with a flock, missionaries exiled at the ends of the earth, must know something of these mysterious intoxications; and when in the bosom of the huge family which their genius has made for them, they must laugh sometimes at those who pity their restless fate and their abstemious life.

Widows

According to Vauvenargues, there are paths in the public gardens haunted mainly by disappointed ambition, by unhappy inventors, by unachieved fame, by broken hearts, by all those tumultuous, imprisoned souls in whom the last rumble of a thunderstorm can be heard, and which keep well away from the insolent and joyful eyes of the holiday-makers. These shadowy retreats are the meeting-place of those who limp through life.

And it is above all to those places that the poet and the philosopher love to direct their eager conjectures. There they are sure to find pasture. For if there is a place they do not deign to visit, it is above all the joys of the rich. That turbulence in the void has nothing that attracts them: whereas they feel themselves irresistibly drawn to everything weak, ruined, sad, orphaned.

An experienced eye is never mistaken. In those rigid or beaten-down features, in those eyes, hollow, gloomy or gleaming with the last flashes of struggle, in those many deep wrinkles, in those slow or jerky steps, it deciphers immediately the innumerable stories of cheated love, or misunderstood devotion, or unrecompensed effort, of hunger and cold endured humbly and in silence.

Have you ever noticed widows on those solitary benches — poor widows? Whether or not they're in mourning it's easy to recognise them. Then, too, there's always something missing in the mourning of the poor, an absence of harmony which makes it more heartbreaking. They have to economise on mourning, whereas the rich wear theirs correct in every detail.

Which is the sadder and more depressing: the widow accompanied by a child with whom she can't share her thoughts, or the widow who is quite alone? I don't know . . . I had occasion once to follow an afflicted old woman of this kind for hours and hours: she was stiff, upright, wearing a little worn-out shawl, her whole being filled with Stoic pride.

She was obviously condemned, through total solitude, to the habits of an old bachelor, and the masculine quality of her behaviour added a strange piquancy to her austerity. I don't know what wretched café she took her meals in, or what she ate. I followed her to the reading room, and I spied on her for a long time while she looked through the papers with active eyes that had been burned by tears, searching for bits of news that had a powerful and personal interest for her.

Finally, in the afternoon, beneath a delightful autumn sky, one of those skies from which regrets and memories descend in showers, she sat down in a corner of the garden to listen, far from the crowd, to one of the concerts which regimental bands put on to gratify the inhabitants of Paris.

This was no doubt the modest indulgence of that innocent (or purified) old lady, the well-earned consolation for one of those dreary days without friends, without conversation, without joy and without confidant, which God has been providing her with, perhaps for many years – 365 times a year!

And here is another:

I can never resist glancing, not always in sympathy, but at least in curiosity, at the crowd of pariahs pressed round the enclosure at a public concert. The orchestra sends out its festive, triumphant or pleasurable tunes into the night. Dresses swirl and catch the light; glances meet; the holiday-makers, worn out with doing nothing, shift from one foot to the other, pretending to savour the music indolently. Wealth and happiness everywhere; everything breathes a carefree air, everything suggests the pleasure of letting yourself go – everything except the appearance of the crowd over there, leaning on the outside of the fence, catching, as the wind passes, an occasional fragment of the free music, and looking at the sparkling furnace within.

The reflection of the pleasures of the rich in the eyes of the poor is always fascinating. But that day I made out, against the people dressed in blouses and muslin, one being whose nobility formed a striking contrast with all the surrounding triviality. It was a tall, majestic woman, with such a noble appearance that I cannot remember ever seeing her equal in the collections of aristocratic beauties of the past. Her whole being gave off a scent of haughty virtue. Her sad, emaciated face was in perfect harmony with the deep mourning she wore. Like the common people she had placed herself among, and whom she took no notice of, she too was watching the luminous world with a profound gaze, and she nodded her head gently as she listened.

Striking vision! You can be sure, I said to myself, that that poverty, if indeed it is poverty, does not allow itself any sordid economies; so noble a face is a guarantee of that. So why does she stay voluntarily in a setting where she forms such a striking contrast?

But as I passed close to her to satisfy my curiosity, I thought I could guess the reason. The tall widow was holding a child by the hand, dressed, like her, in black; modest as the price of entry was, that price would suffice to buy something that the little creature needed, or, better still, an extra, a toy.

And she will have returned home on foot, meditating and dreaming, alone, always alone; for children are rowdy, selfish, unresponsive and impatient; and they can't even manage what an animal can, a dog or a cat for instance, to serve as a confidant for solitary grief.

A Hemisphere of Hair

Let me breathe in the ardour of your hair for a long, long time, let me plunge my face into it, like a thirsty man into the water of a stream; let me shake it about with my hand like a perfumed handkerchief, so that I fill the air with memories.

If you could only know all I see, all I smell, all I hear in your hair! My soul is carried away by that scent as other souls are by music.

Your hair contains a dream, a dream inhabited by sails and masts. It contains great seas where the trade winds carry me off to charming climates, where space is bluer and deeper, where the atmosphere is perfumed by fruits, by leaves and by human skin.

On the ocean of your hair I glimpse a port swarming with melancholy songs, with vigorous men of every nation, and with ships of every shape, their delicate and complicated architecture outlined against an immense sky where everlasting heat struts about.

In the caresses of your hair I recapture the languors of long hours passed on a divan, in the cabin of a beautiful ship, rocked by the imperceptible swell in the harbour, between the vases of flowers and the porous jugs of refreshing water.

On the burning hearth of your hair I breathe the smell of tobacco mixed with opium and sugar; in the night of your hair I see the infinite tropical azure shining. On the downy banks of your hair I grow intoxicated with the blended smell of tar, of musk, and of coconut oil.

Let me go on biting at your heavy black tresses. When I chew at your elastic, rebellious hairs, I seem to be eating memories.

The Eyes of the Poor

Ah! You want to know why I hate you today. It will undoubtedly be harder for you to understand than for me to explain; for you must be the finest example one could find of female impenetrability.

We had passed a long day together which had seemed short to me. We had promised each other that we would share all our thoughts, and that from now on our two souls would be as one; – not a very original dream, after all, even though it is dreamed by all men and achieved by none.

In the evening you were rather tired, and wanted to sit down in a new café on the corner of a new boulevard still covered with debris, which was already displaying its uncompleted splendour. The café was sparkling. The very gas shone with the eagerness of a newcomer, lighting up with all its strength the walls that blinded us with their whiteness, the dazzling surface of the mirrors, the gold of the mouldings and the cornices, the pages with their chubby cheeks dragged along by dogs on a lead, the ladies smiling at a falcon perched on their fist, the nymphs and the goddesses carrying fruits, pâté and game on their heads, the Hebes and the Ganymedes with arms stretched out offering little jars of sweetmeats or an obelisk of multicoloured ices – the whole of history, the whole of mythology, in the service of gluttony.

Right in front of us, on the roadway, stood a worthy man of forty-odd, with a grizzled beard; he looked tired, and held a little boy with one hand, while on the other arm he carried a tiny creature too weak to walk. He was their nursemaid, bringing the children out to take the evening air. They were all in rags. The three faces were strikingly earnest, and the six eyes stared at the new café with the same wonder, but subtly differentiated by age.

The father's eyes said: How beautiful! How beautiful! One would think all the gold in the world had been brought here for these walls. The eyes of the little boy said: How beautiful! How beautiful! But this place is not for the likes of us. As for the eyes of the tiny one, they were too fascinated to express anything other than a deep, stupefied joy.

The cabaret songs tell us that pleasure makes the soul good and softens the heart. The songs were right that evening, as far as I was concerned. I was not only touched by that family of eyes, I felt a bit ashamed of our glasses and our decanters, much more than our thirst required. I turned to look at you, my love, in order to read my own thoughts; I plunged into your eyes, so beautiful and so strangely sweet, into your green eyes inhabited by caprice, inspired by the moon, when you said to me: 'I can't stand those people, with their eyes like wide open gates. Couldn't you ask the manager to get rid of them?'

That's how difficult it is to understand each other, my angel, that's how incommunicable our thoughts are, even between people in love.

The Generous Gambler

Yesterday, among the crowd on the boulevard, I brushed against a mysterious Being I'd always wanted to meet, and whom I recognised immediately, though I'd never seen him before. He must have had a corresponding wish to meet me, since he gave me a meaning wink, which I hastened to obey. I followed him carefully, and soon I was descending after him into a dazzling underground residence, blazing with luxury unequalled by any of the finest homes in Paris. It seemed odd to me that I could so often have passed by such a distinguished lair without noticing it. The atmosphere that reigned there was exquisite, though intoxicating; it banished almost instantly all the burdensome horrors of life; there you breathed in a sombre blessedness, just like that which the lotus eaters must have felt when, landing on an enchanted isle, lit by the gleam of eternal afternoon, hearing the drowsy sounds of melodious waterfalls, they felt a desire never to see their homes, their wives or their children again, never again to ride the high waves of the sea.

There were strange faces of men and women there, touched with fatal beauty: faces which I seemed to have seen before in past ages and in other countries which I can't exactly remember, and which inspired in me a fraternal sympathy rather than the fear which we normally feel at the sight of anything unknown. If I wanted to try and find some way of defining the singular expression in their looks, I'd say that I've never seen eyes shining more energetically with the horror of boredom and the ` immortal desire to feel alive.

My host and I, as we sat down, were already old friends. We ate and drank to excess. There were all sorts of extraordinary wines, and (just as extraordinary) the hours passed and I didn't seem to get any more drunk than he did. But every now and then our frequent libations were interrupted by gambling, that superhuman pleasure, and I must say that I played a set of games and lost my soul with a positively heroic indifference. The soul is so impalpable, so often useless, and sometimes such a nuisance that its loss caused me rather less emotion than if I'd gone for a walk and lost a visiting card.

We sat a good while smoking cigars whose incomparable savour and scent roused in the soul a nostalgia for unknown countries and joys; and, intoxicated with all these delights, I was bold enough, in an excess of familiarity which didn't seem to displease him, to grab hold of a brimming cup and call out, 'To your immortal health, you old goat.'

So we sat chatting about the universe, about its creation and future destruction; about the great idea of our century, that is, progress and perfectibility, and in general every kind of human infatuation. On that topic, His Highness had an inexhaustible fund of entertaining and irrefutable jokes, and he expressed himself with a graceful diction and an amused tranquillity that I've never found in any of the most famous of human storytellers. He explained to me the absurdity of the different philosophies that up to now have occupied human minds, and even condescended to confide to me some fundamental principles which I don't think I ought to share with just anyone. He didn't complain in the slightest about the bad reputation he enjoys in every part of the world, assured me that no one was more interested than he in the destruction of superstition, and confessed to me that the only time he had felt any fear concerning his own power was when he heard a preacher, more subtle than his colleagues, cry out from the pulpit, Dear brethren, never forget that the finest of all the devil's tricks is to persuade you that he doesn't exist.

The remembrance of this famous orator leads naturally to the question of the academy, and my strange host assured me that he did not consider it beneath him to inspire the pen, the spoken word, and the conscience of pedagogues, and that he was almost always present, though invisible, in the classroom.

Encouraged by so much goodness, I asked him for news of God, and if he had seen him lately. He replied with a jauntiness mingled with a touch of sadness: 'We greet each other when we happen to meet, but we're like a couple of elderly gentlemen in whom innate politeness cannot quite extinguish the memory of ancient rancour.'

It's doubtful if His Highness has ever given such a long audience to a simple mortal, and I was afraid of abusing it. At last, as the first gleams of dawn whitened the windows, this celebrated personage, hymned by so many powers and served by so many philosophers who have contributed without realising it to his fame, said to me: 'I'd like you to have a favourable memory of me, and I'd like to prove to you that although people say such bad things about me, I'm sometimes a good old devil (to use one of your popular expressions). And so to make up for the irredeemable loss you've sustained, that of your soul, I'll give you the stake you would have won if luck had gone your way, that is, the ability during your whole life to relieve, indeed to overcome, that strange condition of Boredom which is the source of all your ills and of all your miserable progress. You will never have a desire without my helping you to realise it; you will reign over your vulgar compeers; you will have your fill of flattery and even of adoration; money, gold, diamonds, fairy palaces, will seek you out and will beg you to accept them without your having to make any effort to earn them; you will change from one country and homeland to another just as often as your whim commands; you'll intoxicate yourself with voluptuous delights without getting tired of them, in charming lands where it's always warm, and where the women smell as good as the flowers – etc, etc,' he added, as he rose to bid me farewell with a gracious smile.

If I hadn't been afraid of humiliating him in front of such a large gathering, I would gladly have fallen at the feet of the generous player to thank him for such unheard of munificence. But after I'd left him, an incurable mistrust crept gradually back into my breast; I could no longer believe in such prodigious happiness, and as I went to bed, saying my prayers (a stupid habit I can't shake off) I kept saying, while I was half asleep, 'O God, O Lord God, make the devil keep his word.'

Get Drunk

One should always be drunk. That's the one thing that matters. In order not to feel the horrible burden of Time, which breaks your shoulders and crushes you to the ground, one should be drunk without ceasing.

But on what? On wine, on poetry, or on virtue, as suits you. But get drunk.

And if sometimes, on the steps of a palace, on the green grass of a ditch, in the lonely gloom of your room, you wake up, the drunkenness already abated or completely gone, ask the wind, the wave, the star, the bird, the clock, everything that flies or groans or rolls or sings or speaks, ask everything what time it is; and the wind, the wave, the star, the bird, the clock will answer: 'Time to get drunk. In order not to be the martyred slaves of Time, get drunk. Get drunk ceaselessly. On wine, on poetry, or on virtue, as suits you.'

Beat up the Poor

I'd been confined to my room for a fortnight; and I surrounded myself with books that were then fashionable (it was in 1848) – I mean books dealing with the art of making people happy, wise and rich in twenty-four hours. And so I had digested (or rather, just swallowed) all the laborious conclusions of all those entrepreneurs of public happiness – those who advise the poor to make slaves of themselves, and those who persuade them that they are all dethroned kings. You won't be surprised to learn that I was by then in a state of mind not far from vertigo or stupidity.

The one thing I seemed to feel, stuck somewhere at the back of my mind, was the obscure germ of an idea that was superior to all I'd found in that dictionary of the formulae of well-meaning women which I'd just been running through. But it was only the idea of an idea, something infinitely vague.

I emerged with a raging thirst: for a passionate taste for bad books causes a proportionate need for open air and refreshments.

As I was entering a restaurant, a beggar held out his hat with one of those unforgettable looks which could overthrow thrones if mind could move matter, and if the eye of a mesmeriser could cause grapes to ripen.

At the same time I heard a voice whispering in my ear, a voice I recognised well: it was that of the good angel – or good devil – who accompanies me everywhere. Since Socrates had his good Demon, why shouldn't I have my good angel, and why shouldn't I have the honour, like Socrates, of having my diploma in madness, signed by the best people?

There is one difference between Socrates' Demon and mine: his only appeared to him in order to forbid, to warn, and to prevent, whereas mine is willing to advise, to suggest and to persuade. Poor Socrates only had a prohibiting Demon; mine is a great affirmer, mine is a Demon of action, a Demon of combat. And now his voice whispered to me: 'No one is the equal of another unless he can prove it; the only one worthy of liberty is he who knows how to conquer it.'

And immediately I leaped on my beggar. With one blow of my fist I punched his eye, which swelled up in a moment as big as a tennis ball. I damaged one of my nails in breaking two of his teeth, and since I was born delicate, and don't practise boxing much, and so didn't consider myself strong enough to give the old man a quick knock-out, I grabbed him by the collar with one hand, seized his throat with the other, and began banging his head vigorously against a wall. I have to admit that I had previously glanced round the neighbourhood (it was a deserted suburb) to make sure that I would be safely out of the reach of the police for as long as I needed.

Then, by means of a kick in the back strong enough to break his shoulderblades, I knocked down the feeble sexagenarian, and grabbing hold of a large branch which was lying on the ground, I beat him with the obstinate energy of a cook tenderising a beefsteak.

Suddenly – O miracle, O delight of a philosopher verifying the excellence of his theory – I saw that ancient carcass turn round, straighten up with an energy I'd never have suspected in such a broken-down machine, and with a look of hatred that seemed to me to augur well, the decrepit old ruffian threw himself at me, blackened both my eyes, broke four of my teeth, and with the same branch began showering blows on me. My vigorous treatment had given him back both pride and life.

Then I made signs to indicate to him that I considered the discussion at an end, and pulling myself up with the satisfaction of a Stoic philosopher, said to him: 'You are my equal! Do me the honour of sharing my money with me; and if you are a real philanthropist, remember to try out on all your colleagues, when they demand alms from you, the theory that I've just had the painful experience of trying on you.'

He assured me that he had understood my theory, and would follow my advice.

Chronology of Baudelaire's Life

Year	Age	Life
1821		Born 9 April
1827	6	Death of Baudelaire's father, aged 66 (his mother was then 33)
1828	7	His mother marries Commander (later General) Aupick. Critics with a taste for psychoanalytical explanations have seen in this family situation the origins of his irregular life, his sexual licence and his contempt for the bourgeoisie
1839	18	Expelled from college (for a minor offence)
1841	20	His family, disturbed by his Bohemian life, send him on a voyage to India; he only gets as far as Mauritius and Réunion
1842	21	Returns to France. Begins his lifelong liaison with Jeanne Duval, the mulatto woman to whom he wrote most of his love poems
1843	22	By now, Baudelaire is writing poetry in earnest. Many of his poems that were published much later date from this time
1844	23	Disturbed by his extravagance, his mother and stepfather place his finances under the control of a notary. From now on, he is never out of debt

Chronology of his Times

Year	Literary Context	Historical Events
1820	Lamartine, *Méditations poétiques*	
1821	Death of Keats	
1822	Death of Shelley	
1826	Vigny, *Poèmes antiques et modernes*	
1827	Hugo, *Cromwell*	
1830	Lamartine, *Harmonies Poétiques* Tennyson, *Poems, Chiefly Lyrical*	July Revolution in France. Louis-Philippe becomes the 'roi-citoyen'
1831	Hugo, *Notre Dame de Paris* Stendhal, *le Rouge et le Noir*	In England George IV dies, William IV crowned
1833	Robert Browning, *Pauline*	
1834	Death of Coleridge Musset, *Lorenzaccio* Balzac, *le Père Goriot*	
1835	Vigny, *Chatterton* de Tocqueville, *Democracy in America*	
1836	Dickens, *Sketches by Boz*	
1837	Balzac, *Illusions perdues* Carlyle, *The French Revolution*	Death of William IV in England; Victoria crowned
1839	Stendhal, *la Chartreuse de Parme*	
1842	Tennyson, *Poems* Death of Stendhal	

Year	Age	Life
1845	24	*Salon de 1845* published – first of his art criticism, containing high praise of Delacroix Attempts suicide
1846	25	*Salon de 1846* published: a more interesting piece of art criticism
1847	26	*Fanfarlo* (a short novel) published
1848	27	During the 1848 revolution he displayed a brief enthusiasm for revolutionary politics, and was seen on the barricades threatening to shoot General Aupick First of his many translations of Poe published
1851	30	Essay on wine and hashish (a sketch for *les Paradis artificiels*) and nine poems published in the *Messager de l'Assemblée*
1852	31	First essay on Poe published. Beginning of the friendship with Mme Sabatier, to whom he addresses (anonymously) a series of poems
1853	32	Translations of several of Poe's *Tales* published
1855	34	Three articles on the Universal Exhibition published. Eighteen poems published in the *Revue des deux mondes* under the title *les Fleurs du mal* (Flowers of Evil)
1856	35	Translation of Poe's *Tales* published Breaks with Jeanne Duval
1857	36	Death of General Aupick *les Fleurs du mal* published. It is attacked in *le Figaro* ('Nothing can justify a man of more than thirty years of age in publishing such monstrosities'). It is then seized by the police, placed on trial, and condemned. Baudelaire fined and ordered to suppress six poems. Victor Hugo praises the book enthusiastically

Year	Literary Context	Historical Events
1845	Poe, *Tales* Mérimée, *Carmen*	
1846	The Brontës, *Poems*	
1847	Charlotte Brontë, *Jane Eyre*	
1848	Thackeray, *Vanity Fair*	Revolution in France; abdication of Louis-Philippe
1850	Elizabeth Browning, *Sonnets From the Portuguese* Dickens, *David Copperfield* Tennyson, *In Memoriam* Death of Balzac	
1851	Hugo goes into exile in the Channel Islands	In France coup d'état of Louis Napoleon The Great Exhibition in London
1852	Matthew Arnold, *Poems* Lecomte de Lisle, *Poèmes antiques* Gautier, *Emaux et Camées*	In France Louis Napoleon becomes Napoleon III; beginning of the Second Empire
1854	Nerval, *les Filles du Feu*	The Crimean War (1853–6)
1855	Robert Browning, *Men and Women*	
1857	Flaubert, *Madame Bovary* Elizabeth Browning, *Aurora Leigh*	

Year	Age	Life
1858	37	His translation of Poe's *Arthur Gordon Pym* published
		Reunited with Jeanne Duval. Despite constant quarrels, they do not again separate
1859	38	*le Voyage*, the longest of his poems, written and published
		Salon de 1859 published in *la Revue française*
1860	39	*les Paradis artificiels* published
1861	40	Second edition of *les Fleurs du mal*, with thirty-five new poems
		Richard Wagner and Tannhäuser, an essay which praises Wagner enthusiastically
		Begins to publish prose poems, which appear in various periodicals over the next few years
		Unsuccessful candidature for a vacant place in the Académie française
1863	42	Essay on Delacroix
		le Peintre de la vie moderne (The Painter of Modern Life), his essay on Constantin Guys: the finest of all his works of art criticism
1864	43	*le Figaro*, after publishing six of his prose poems under the title *le Spleen de Paris* (which became the eventual title of the collection), refuses to publish any more because, according to the editor, 'everyone is bored by them'
		Moves to Brussels, where he was to deliver a series of lectures; these were a flop. Despite his contempt for Belgium (expressed vigorously in his book *Pauvre Belgique*), he stays there for most of the short remainder of his life
1865	44	His health steadily deteriorates
1866	45	Wins enthusiastic praise from the young poets Mallarmé and Verlaine
		Suffers a stroke, from which he never really recovers. His mother comes to Belgium to nurse him
		Sixteen poems in *le Parnasse contemporain* under the title 'Nouvelles Fleurs du Mal'
1867	46	After a long and painful illness, he dies in his mother's arms on 31 August

Year	Literary Context	Historical Events
1858	George Eliot, *Scenes of Clerical Life*	
1859	Tennyson, *Idylls of the King*	
1860	George Eliot, *The Mill on the Floss*	
1862	Hugo, *les Misérables*	
1863	Renan, *Life of Jesus* Death of Vigny	

Year	Age	Life
1868		Third edition of *les Fleurs du mal* published
1869		*l'Art Romantique* and *Petits Poèmes en Prose* published
1887		Publication of *Fusées* (Rockets) and *Mon Coeur mis à nu* (My Heart Laid Bare), two collections of jottings and intimate self-revelations